HEADGEAR

HEADGEAR

by Ron Hirschi Photographs by Galen Burrell

DODD, MEAD & COMPANY NEW YORK

For
Brenda, Jean,
and Nichol

1   2   3   4   5   6   7   8   9   10

Library of Congress Cataloging-in-Publication Data
Hirschi, Ron
    Headgear.
    Includes index.
    Summary: Discusses the characteristics and habitats of horned and
antlered North American animals, such as elk, bighorn, pronghorn, moose,
caribou, deer, and mountain goat, and presents some of the folklore
associated with these animals' headgear.
    1. Horns—Juvenile literature. 2. Antlers—Juvenile literature. 3. Bovidae
—Juvenile literature. 4. Cervidae—Juvenile literature. 5. Mammals—North
America—Juvenile literature. [1. Horns 2. Antlers 3. Bovidae. 4.
Cervidae. 5. Zoology—North America] I. Burrell, Galen, ill. II. Title.
QL942.H57 1986   599.73'5   85-20407
ISBN 0-396-08673-X

CONTENTS

INTRODUCTION

As wildlife biologists, we have spent many hours observing elk, deer, moose, bison, bighorn sheep, mountain goats, and pronghorns. It is our hope that this book, which explores the natural history of North American animals with horns and antlers, will impart our feeling for these and other animals to you so that we all will help to insure their continued survival.

You can see how each animal uses its headgear to survive and how horns and antlers differ, depending on where the animal lives.

Throughout the book we have attempted to invite the reader to enter into the landscape occupied by each animal. Color photographs add greatly to the window on the world of the elk, pronghorn, and other antlered and horned animals.

ELK MEADOW

Follow a bull elk on his path through a late winter snowfall. A soft hush fills the air as his hooves cut through the thin crust of snow. His trail leads down the mountain to a broad meadow in the Rocky Mountain foothills. Here he stops and, with a twisting shake of his head, his wide-branched antlers fall to the ground.

But the old bull isn't harmed when he sheds his headgear. He has endured many winter storms. He has also grown and shed several sets of antlers during his lifetime. As in years past, each set of antlers helped keep his body cool in summer, clashed with other bull's headgear during the mating season, and served as a symbol of strength among members of the elk herd. Having served their purpose for this year, the antlers are no longer needed and the old bull spends the remainder of winter without them.

Bull elk in the snow.

Elk antlers shed in the foothills of the Rocky Mountains. This view shows the base of the antler bone where it was attached to the pedicle.

When winter ends, the bull will retrace his path up the mountain where glacier lilies will poke through the snow now blanketing the meadow. Mice will gnaw on the discarded antlers and, in time, the headgear will become a part of the mountain soil. The old bull's new antlers will emerge from two permanent bases called pedicles, just as the glacier lilies emerge from their bulbs each spring.

A new antler grows from each pedicle. Like all antlers, they are made of bone and covered with a temporary layer of skin as soft as velvet. This velvet layer supplies nourishing blood to the growing bone and protects the delicate new set of headgear.

The elk's new antlers grow rapidly. They are a heavy burden, even for the strongest bull in the herd.

Close view of velvet-covered antlers.

But the extra weight is tolerated, even during the heat of summer, since the velvet-covered antlers are a convenient cooling system.

On hot summer days, gentle breezes blow against the antlers, cooling blood that flows through the velvet skin. Just as cold lemonade refreshes you, the cool blood refreshes the elk as the fluid circulates from antlers to the rest of his body.

Young bull elk wear smaller antlers than older males.

Much smaller headgear is worn by young bull elk. A bull's first set emerges at one year of age and does not branch like the antlers of mature bulls.

As yearlings, young bulls chase one another. They play-fight with their antlers as if pirates flashing bright new swords. As adults, the bulls won't have to fight so often or so violently, since they learn to respect the strength of others during their play-fights.

By the time aspen leaves turn golden and fall to the forest floor, elk antlers stop growing and begin to

Young bulls, antler-to-antler.

harden. Blood no longer flows through the velvet and the sheath of skin dries like grass stems in the meadow.

Completely hardened and fully grown, an elk's headgear is no longer sensitive to touch. Only bulls wear antlers and they rub their headgear against shrubs and small trees to remove the irritating sheaths that itch like sunburned skin. Saplings are stripped of bark, branches broken, and leaves shredded. But this commotion serves a purpose; bulls learn the shapes of

Snow flies as a bull elk thrashes vegetation at the beginning of the fall mating season.

The bull is able to run through thick vegetation because he learned the shape of his antlers while shrub thrashing.

their headgear by rubbing against plants. If chased by predators, bulls can run through the forest without tangling their antlers in the trees because they have learned this valuable lesson.

When mating season begins, bugling calls echo through crisp fall air as bulls announce their presence to rival males. Those with a herd of cows stand ready, their headgear serving as symbols of strength. When challenged by other males, larger and stronger bulls with superior headgear easily chase off the intruders.

Occasionally, the clash of antlers echoes down the mountainside when bulls of equal strength fight for a herd of cows. But head-to-head combat rarely ends in serious battle or injury, since weaker animals yield to dominant bulls.

Bugling bull surrounded by his herd of cows.

A fight for dominance by two bulls. After a brief clash of antlers, the victor chases off his rival.

Bull elk with his herd of cows.

When mating season ends, younger members of the elk herd end their year by following the path of the older bulls. In a late winter snowfall, young males drop their headgear one or two weeks after the stronger males shed theirs. Bare as the leafless branches of winter aspen, the bulls, young and old, descend the mountain to begin a new year in the meadows below.

Bluebirds resting on a patch of melting snow are the first sign of warm seasons to come.

BIGHORNS' MOUNTAIN

Spring comes slowly to the bighorns' mountain. Far below, winter has passed and elk graze in the broad meadow along the river. Here in the high country, bluebirds resting on a patch of melting snow are the first sign of warm seasons to come.

Where snow has already blown free, bighorn rams gather in all-male groups to feed. Their horns sweep back in elegant curls and their stout bodies fit the landscape well. Like weathered stones, these sheep are a part of the windswept ridges and, hopefully, a part of the mountain's future.

Bighorn headgear is also like a stone. It may become chipped, broken, or worn, but it is never shed like an elk antler. True horn, sheep headgear has a central core of bone that is permanently attached to the bighorn's skull. Surrounding this bone core is a covering made of keratin. Unlike an antler's tempo-

A group of male bighorns.

rary layer of soft, velvet skin, this keratin layer is tough and permanent.

Keratin is the substance commonly known as horn. It is the same substance that forms a bird's beak, a cat's claws, and your fingernails.

If you look closely at a bighorn ram's headgear, you will see growth rings. These rings form each winter when growth slows, then stops. In spring the bone core and its keratin sheath grow longer and wider. This new growth pushes outward, gradually forming a spiral. You can see each year's growth separated by the winter rings and use each band to estimate the age of a bighorn ram.

Close view of the bighorn ram's horns.

This bighorn ram is four or five years old.

A ram learns the many pathways on its mountain home by following other sheep. It first enters the intimate world of male sheep society during its second year. Before that time it travels nearby slopes with a band of ewes, yearlings, and lambs. When he leaves them behind, the young ram follows older bighorns to their traditional wintering grounds.

During the next three to five years, the young ram continues to follow the lead of older rams that wear larger headgear. He learns new paths to summer, winter, and breeding grounds. He also learns to

Horn-to-horn nuzzling. Bighorns live in close contact with one another through the year.

recognize other members of the herd by their horn size, scent, and overall appearance. Constant sparring, shoving matches, and head-to-head nuzzling communicate his rank and status within the sheep society.

Gradually, the ram increases his dominance. As his horns grow, he is able to successfully lead other males to traditional feeding grounds. His larger horns also give him greater advantage when challenged for a mate by unfamiliar rams that travel to his breeding grounds from distant slopes.

Two ewes, two lambs, and a yearling ram.

Unlike elk, bighorn rams do not tend a herd of females. Instead, they mate with ewes that gather on the breeding grounds, where several males compete for the attention of the females. The ewes also wear headgear. Although their horns are smaller than the rams', females use them effectively.

When her lamb is born, the ewe keeps a close watch over her young one. Arching her head and horns toward intruders, she keeps unwelcome sheep at a distance. This horn threat is as well understood in sheep society as the shaking of a fist or an angry shout is in human society.

Bighorn rams also face intruders with horn threats. Males seem to know one another's strength and rank, based on a quick glance. In most cases the less-dominant, shorter-horned ram submits during these encounters.

During the breeding season, challenges may lead to horn-to-horn battles. When two rams crash head-to-head, they are well equipped for defense. The rams' horns seem best adapted to protect both combatants rather than to inflict injury. The massive headgear cushions severe blows. An air-filled network of bone chambers in the skull further shields the ram's brain—like a head protector worn by an Olympic boxer.

But protection for sheep society is incomplete. Bighorn headgear is an attractive trophy and the largest horns are highly valued by human hunters. If old rams are killed before passing on their knowledge of how to travel their traditional pathways, sheep herds suffer severe disruptions. With protection, young rams will be able to follow their leaders. Then bighorns will always be a part of the windswept ridges when bluebirds return to the mountain in springs to come.

Rams following other male bighorns to traditional winter feeding grounds.

HORNS
OR ANTLERS?

Warm rays of sun break the chill of early morning on the prairie stretching to the east of the bighorns' mountain. No trees grow on this dry grassland. The low hills rise and fall in gentle waves and the crest of a distant ridge is broken only by the outline of a herd of pronghorns.

The herd stands alert.

If a coyote breaks the endless edge between sky and prairie, the sharp-eyed pronghorns will see this predator long before it spots the herd. When alarmed, lookouts signal to grazing members by fluffing the white hairs on their rump patches. The fastest North American land mammals, pronghorns also warn others with coughing snorts, then vanish at speeds approaching fifty miles per hour.

Klamath Indians were well attuned to the pronghorns' vocal signals. They called these prairie dwell-

Pronghorns are the fastest North American land mammals.

Prairie dogs share the pronghorn's home.

ers *Cha-oo*, in imitation of the sound pronghorns make when about to run.

Our name for the pronghorn comes from the short branches, or prongs, on the male's headgear. But is its unusual headgear horn or antler? Actually it is neither, having features common to both.

Like bighorn sheep, bison, and other horned animals, both male and female pronghorns wear headgear. It is not known why, but females occasionally lack theirs. When present, the doe's headgear is spikelike and usually less than three inches long. Typ-

30

Our name for the pronghorns comes from the short branches or prongs on the male's headgear.

Coyotes are among the pronghorn's predators.

A doe's headgear is spikelike.

ically curving back, then turning slightly inward, the buck's headgear branches once. His prongs are a prominent feature on his sleek frame.

During head-to-head battles for control of small herds of does, the buck's prongs protect his face. The prongs block an opponent's stabbing motions, preventing the sharp horn tips from inflicting injury.

Like elk, deer, and other antlered animals, pronghorns shed their headgear each winter. But

32

they drop only the outer keratin sheaths, prongs included. The sheaths slip off and drop among the sage growing on windswept ridges that pronghorns follow to avoid deep snow. When their headgear sheds, the bone cores still remain. These cores look like cones or icicles pointing skyward and are permanently attached to the pronghorns' skulls.

The bone cores of a pronghorn's headgear form the bases for new keratin growth. The new year's layer of keratin begins slowly in winter. By spring, a new set of headgear is fully formed. It grows larger than that worn the previous year and commands greater respect among herd members.

A sheath among the sage.

FROZEN NORTH

A hawk circles high above the winter prairie. It dips past pronghorn herds, flies over the high ridges of the bighorns' mountain, then glides above the river's path. Winter will soon pass and the hawk has begun its long migration to northern nesting grounds. Far below, a cow moose browses willows along the streambank.

The moose pays no attention to the shadow cast by the hawk and she feels no migratory urge. Although some moose travel twenty miles or more between summer and winter feeding grounds, many are like this cow. She stays near the sound of flowing water.

In late May, she gives birth to a calf, weighing 25 to 35 pounds, at the edge of the stream. The calf stays close beside its highly protective mother throughout the summer. Growing more rapidly than

Cow moose with calf.

almost all other land mammals, the long-legged calf may weigh 250 pounds by autumn and 400 to 600 pounds by the following spring. By then, a yearling male wears tiny, buttonlike antlers. This first set and future antlers worn by the moose emerge from pedicles like that of the elk. The antlers, like others, are made of bone and covered with a layer of skin.

Female yearlings, like all cow moose and cow elk, normally lack headgear. Regardless of sex, all yearlings are driven off by their mothers shortly before the cows give birth to their new calves. This sudden independence is confusing for young moose. Many yearlings stay within sight of their mothers as their second summer begins, but the cows remain in-

Young bull moose.

Bull moose removing antler velvet.

tolerant and approaches much closer than 100 yards may result in threatening kicks from sharp hooves.

Unlike cows, bull moose tolerate youngsters throughout the warm summer. But moose form no permanent herds and the bonds between these temporary summer groups are weak. When velvet begins to peel from the bull's scoop-shaped antlers, all intruding males are driven off as the mating season begins.

Adult bull moose.

During the mating season, bulls battle antler-to-antler. But their headgear are not effective weapons. They serve best as symbols of strength and communicate a well-understood message. Like young lieutenants, small antlered males respect the status of old bull moose as if they were generals in command of an army.

Females also respond to the bull's antler size. They are attracted to a male with large headgear and also follow an attracting scent the male spreads in a shallow excavation, or wallow. He digs the wallow with his hooves and his antler scoops. Then the pair often lie together as part of their brief courtship.

After little more than a week of close attention, the cow is abandoned by her mate and returns to her solitary life along the river.

Bull moose may court more than one female during the fall mating season. But long before his antlers drop in winter, he retreats to the spruce woods, a secluded meadow, or a marsh hidden in the north woods. His winter is spent in solitude and his head remains antlerless until next spring. Until then his pedicles look like bald spots and it is hard to imagine that each year he will grow a new set of antlers that spread as wide as six feet.

Bull moose. His antlers have just dropped, revealing the pedicle.

Musk-ox. Like all horned animals, the headgear of the musk-ox is not shed each year.

Much farther north, herds of shaggy musk-oxen huddle together to face the fierce cold of arctic nights. With young in the center of the group, musk-oxen form a tight circle, facing outward, to protect their offspring from the wind. Above their bare noses and dark eyes, pairs of true horns sweep outward from bone shields covering their foreheads.

Antlered caribou share the musk-oxen's home in the frozen north. Their headgear also shares something in common with these and all other horned animals. Unlike any other antlered animal in the world, most female caribou wear headgear.

Females wear smaller antlers than those worn by males, but cows use their headgear to help them survive.

Snow often covers the caribou's summer feeding grounds when the herds first return from a winter in forests to the south. The caribou must scratch through the cold surface to reach lichens and other food plants growing on the tundra. Competition for feeding space is often severe in herds that might number in the thousands. This competition between herd members does not occur among moose, elk, or other antlered animals. Since caribou cows must compete with males to survive, their struggle for food is thought to be responsible for their need for headgear.

Male caribou shed their intricately branched antlers in winter. Since cows keep their headgear until spring, females are able to chase the defenseless bulls from valuable feeding areas. This ensures that females obtain adequate food for themselves at a crucial time. More importantly for the survival of the en-

tire herd, pregnant cows are ensured food that is needed to nourish their developing young.

By the time calves are born, female caribou have shed their antlers and a new cycle of life begins. In contrast to their silence during the arctic winter and long migrations, the summer is greeted with much bellowing and softer calls from young caribou searching for their mothers.

Although days are long, the arctic summer passes quickly. Soon, the long migration to wintering grounds begins. By then, bulls and cows have re-grown their antlers and they gather in herds that head into the wind.

When the arctic breeze blows against its antlers, a caribou turns to follow a path with the least wind resistance. Even though each caribou wears a distinctive set of headgear, the general shape and angle to the wind is the same for all herd members and they turn together. Like fixed rudders on a flotilla of sailing ships, their antlers are thought to help steer the caribou on a common southern course.

Caribou Unlike all other antlered animals,
both male and female caribou wear headgear.

TWO OF A KIND

The fragrant scent of ponderosa pine drifts on a gentle breeze. The light wind stirs overhead branches, bends golden stems of grass, and sets the tapered tips of shrubs in motion. But some of the branches tucked behind the shrubs do not move. These "branches" are attached to a deer.

The deer's branched antlers, spread behind the shrubs, help camouflage the buck. He naps in the late afternoon, chewing his cud as he keeps a watchful eye on the open hillside. Should the scent of a predator mingle with the odor of pine, he will be ready.

Like elk and moose, only male deer wear headgear. Their antlers are covered with velvet while growing and secrete an oily substance thought to act as sunburn protection or insect repellent. The antlers harden in the fall and drop each winter.

Perhaps the most familiar of all animals that wear

A deer tucked behind the shrubs.

Buck deer in velvet. The velvet skin protects the growing antlers and provides nourishing blood flow.

headgear, deer are widespread in North America. You could probably describe a deer or draw its picture without looking at photographs. You may have even seen a deer bounding through the woods.

But did you know there are two species of deer

native to North America? Headgear shape is one good way to tell one from the other.

The mule deer's antlers rise abruptly, treelike. Each time a branch is formed, the branches fork in pairs.

This is much different from the white-tailed buck's antlers. The single, main beams of his antlers arch forward as though bent by a constant breeze. Branches rise from the main beam, but they don't fork like those of the mule deer.

Mule deer bucks and a single doe.

Mule deer buck.

White-tailed buck.

Mule deer can be distinguished from whitetails in many other ways. Like their namesakes, mule deer generally have large ears. White-tailed deer have longer, bushier tails with white edges and underparts. The mule deer's black-tipped tails led some North American Indians to call them black-tailed deer. This name persists in the Pacific Northwest where a darker and somewhat smaller mule deer inhabits wet, coastal forests.

Watch closely the next time you see a deer. Its tail will be one clue to its identity. If a buck, its headgear will point to the answer. But remember that no two deer are ever the same. Like people and other animals, each mule deer and each white-tailed deer is an individual. Try as you might, you will never find two alike.

Mule deer buck.

MYTH AND MAGIC

The setting sun sends streaks of purple dancing across the face of the highest mountains. These majestic peaks loom over the forest home of elk and deer, and rise even higher than the windswept ridges of the bighorns' mountain. Here in the steep cliffs, mountain goats live in a land above the clouds.

The mountain goat stares down from its lofty perch as if the ruler of this mountain kingdom. Its shiny horns glisten like jeweled crowns and their sharp tips pierce the crisp evening air. As symbols of strength and as effective weapons, the goat's horns help it survive in this alpine landscape.

Long ago, the mountain goat's headgear was also a valuable possession to the Tlingit people of the Pacific Northwest. The ebony horns were shaped into spoons, then carved in great detail. These horn spoons were practical utensils. Like the finest silver,

Mountain goat.

they were also considered as objects of wealth and are among the most beautiful art created from natural materials.

Headgear of other animals was also fashioned into objects of great value. Elk antlers became knife handles, wedges, and scrapers. Caribou antlers were used by Eskimos as shovels, as fish spears, and as knives to cut snow blocks. Sheep horns were used as ceremonial bowls by the Lakota Indians, and bison horns were a major item in the daily life of people living on the Great Plains.

More importantly, horned and antlered animals themselves were the lifeblood of most North American Indians. Animals provided food, clothing, and shelter. Animals also shared the same spirit Indian people believed flowed through all living things.

Gods controlled these spirits. To the Pawnee of the Great Plains, Tirawa reigned supreme from his position above the clouds. He and his wife controlled lesser gods such as Evening Star, who kept a mythical garden with lush fields of corn. Many bison lived in Evening Star's garden and the Pawnee called upon spirits in the wind to sweep the bison herds to their land along the Platte River.

Kiowa Indians shared many of the Pawnee be-

Mountain goat. The horns of the mountain goat were used by Northwest Coast Indians.

Bison horns were a major feature in the daily life of people living on the Great Plains.

56

liefs. In their solemn and majestic Sun Dance, they placed bison headgear in sacred positions above altar poles. The bison used in the ceremony had been killed by an honored warrior. At one point in the preparations for the ceremony, this Kiowa warrior offered this prayer to the spirit of the Sun:

Sun, look at me.
Let our women and children multiply,
Let buffalo cover the earth,
Let sickness disappear.

Just as spirits in the wind or sun might control animal movements, many Indians believed that animal spirits could influence humans. To the Blackfoot Indians, a pronghorn's spirit could heal the sick. This belief is thought to be based on the pronghorn's ability to renew its headgear each year. Calling on this mysterious ability, Blackfoot medicine men held their hands to their heads in imitation of the pronghorn and danced, in hopes that the sick person would renew his or her strength.

This belief in the restoration power within horns and antlers was widespread in North America. The belief in this magical power persists today in cultures throughout the world.

In Asia, rhinoceros horn is thought to be a cure for many conditions, including jaundice, fever, and skin disease. Turned to a powder or used for knife handles, the unusual and increasingly rare horn of the rhino sells for as much as $20,000 per kilogram (2.2 pounds). Unfortunately, these high prices have led to such great demand that rhinos have been hunted to near extinction for the magical powers of their horns.

Rhinoceros. Although damaged, the rhino's horn will grow back.

Mountain goat in purple light.

Only with protection and understanding will the rhino and other animals with headgear be saved. They all depend on horns and antlers for their own survival. This is true no matter where they live, in the forests, northern tundra, meadow, or high above the bighorns' mountain where a young mountain goat gazes into its future from its home above the clouds.

GLOSSARY

Alpine high mountainous areas above the limits of tree growth.

Antler headgear made of bone that is covered with skin while growing. Antlers are shed each year.

Browse to feed by nibbling tree and shrub branches.

Cud plant food chewed a second time.

Graze to feed by nibbling grass and other low-growing plants.

Horn permanent headgear with a bone base and keratin covering.

Keratin a tough animal fiber made of protein. This word is based on the Greek word for horn, *keras*.

Lichen a kind of plant that is really two plants in one. Lichens are composed of a fungus and an alga that live together.

Pedicle permanent bone base of antlers.

Species a single kind of plant or animal.

Tundra a vast expanse of treeless vegetation in the far north where the ground is always frozen at the surface or a few inches below.

INDEX